NEGOTIATION

(Two Book Box Set)

RYAN JAMES

© **Copyright 2017 by Ryan James - All rights reserved.**

The following Book is reproduced below with the goal of providing information that is as accurate and as reliable as possible. Regardless, purchasing this Book can be seen as consent to the fact that both the publisher and the author of this book are in no way experts on the topics discussed within, and that any recommendations or suggestions made herein are for entertainment purposes only. Professionals should be consulted as needed before undertaking any of the action endorsed herein.

This declaration is deemed fair and valid by both the American Bar Association and the Committee of Publishers Association and is legally binding throughout the United States.

Furthermore, the transmission, duplication or reproduction of any of the following work, including precise information, will be considered an illegal act, irrespective whether it is done electronically or in print. The legality extends to creating a secondary or tertiary copy of the work or a recorded copy and is only allowed with express written consent of the Publisher. All additional rights are reserved.

The information in the following pages is broadly considered to be a truthful and accurate account of facts, and as such any inattention, use or misuse of the information in question by the reader will render any resulting actions solely under their purview. There are no scenarios in which the publisher or the original author of this work can be in any fashion deemed liable for any hardship or damages that may befall them after undertaking information described herein.

Additionally, the information found on the following pages is intended for informational purposes only and should thus be considered, universal. As befitting its nature, the information presented is without assurance regarding its continued validity or interim quality. Trademarks that mentioned are done without written consent and can in no way be considered an endorsement from the trademark holder.

Table of Contents

PERSUASION: The Complete Step by Step Guide on Persuasion, Mind Control and NLP 1

Introduction 3

CHAPTER 1: Persuasion 5

CHAPTER 2: Mind Control 10

CHAPTER 3: NLP 13

CHAPTER 4: Execution 18

CHAPTER 5: Examples 40

CHAPTER 6: Troubleshooting 57

Conclusion 68

Manipulation: The Complete Step-by-Step Guide on Manipulation, Mind Control, and NLP 73

Introduction 75

CHAPTER 1: Manipulating the Mind through NLP 77

CHAPTER 2: Step #1—Building Rapport vs. Fear 92

CHAPTER 3: Step #2—Defining Desired Outcomes 104

CHAPTER 4: Step #3—Considering the Consequences 118

CHAPTER 5: Step #4—Be the Solution to their Problem 129

CHAPTER 6: Step #5— Assuming Success 140

Conclusion 148

PERSUASION:

The Complete Step by Step Guide on Persuasion, Mind Control and NLP

INTRODUCTION

Congratulations and thank you for purchasing *"Persuasion:* The Complete Step by Step Guide on Persuasion, Mind Control and NLP."

This book teaches you how to tap into your inner strength and embrace it so you can effectively accomplish anything you desire to do. Understanding the techniques associated with persuasion, mind control and NLP will assist you in accomplishing any goal you desire, whether it be within' yourself or with the assistance of another person. The best part is, you *already possess this strength.* All you need to do is learn how to tap into it, and use it effectively!

Inside the chapters of this book, you are going to learn exactly how you can tap into these strengths and successfully create your desired life. You will learn exactly what persuasion, mind control and NLP are and how they can help you in your life. Additionally, you will learn exactly how you can use these assets to design your life to be exactly as you desire. Finally, if you are feeling under confident or unsure as to whether or not you are being completely effective in your practice, we have provided excellent sources of information to help you troubleshoot and achieve optimal success with your persuasion, mind control and NLP techniques.

As you may know, there are several books on the market that cover the topics we cover here. Thank you again for choosing this one over the others, and I hope it provides you with enough value to exceed your expectations and assist you in mastering your skills. A significant amount of planning and detail went into creating this book in order to ensure that it would provide you with the most detailed instruction on how you can use these techniques right away. Enjoy!

CHAPTER 1

Persuasion

Persuasion is a technique wherein you encourage someone to think along the same lines as you are and develop the same conclusions. Without persuasion, you run the risk of people formulating their own opinions that may differ from yours, which will quickly cause them to resist what you are saying. If you do not use persuasion, you essentially give people the permission to think whatever they like about your ideas.

In order to better understand persuasion, let's think about a theoretical scenario for a minute. Let's say you are talking to someone about a business proposition. You tell them all of the juicy details and then leave them to their own devices. They're interested, but instead of returning to you, they turn to the person who is easiest to contact in that moment. Perhaps you're unavailable, out of the office, or the conversation started naturally and geared towards that topic. If you failed to use persuasion, the person you proposed your business idea to may decide to go with someone else, instead.

Alternatively, if you were to use persuasion techniques in your pitch, this person would not seek information from other sources in order to make a decision. Instead, they would pursue you for the information, and request that you share more with them. You will have comfortably lead them to the decision, and they will happily hear what you have to say. Instead of immediately thinking the business idea is bad, or feeling that they need to do more research before they commit, they will have trust in you and therefore they will believe you when you tell them it is a good idea. Ideally, they will take the "bait" and go along with whatever idea you have proposed.

When you are using persuasion techniques effectively, the people you are talking to are going to feel as though *they* are in charge of their own thoughts. In reality, they *are.* However, you are using the art of persuasion to guide their thoughts in a direction that is more effective for you in what you are desiring to accomplish. Even though they feel like they are calling the shots, the reality is that *you* are. The best way persuasion works is when you use subliminal persuasion techniques on someone. If you are too aggressive, you may turn them off of your ideas and prevent them from wanting to work with you. That is why learning the art of persuasion properly is so important. The better you are with this art, the easier it will be for you, and the more positive your results will be.

If you are *really* good at what you do, you can actually disagree with someone else without making them feel as though you actually disagree with what they're saying. In fact, you can use these techniques to take someone who is currently disagreeing with you and encourage them to instead agree with you.

The reason why persuasion is so important is because you need to get people agreeing with you.

In order to do this, you need to make sure that you are also agreeing with them. Simply put, this is using the law of attraction. Like things attract like things. In other words, if you are agreeing with someone else, even if you actually don't, you are showing them that you are on the same page as they are, even if you're not. This will help you guide them over to your page, so that instead of them leading the conversation, you are.

Let's investigate a theoretical example to see how persuasion would work in order to take someone who is currently disagreeing and encourage them to agree, instead. Imagine you are trying to make a sale, but the person is resisting. They say, "I don't know how to use this product." You say, "I agree, it can be hard to learn new things sometimes! Luckily, we have an excellent service that allows you the opportunity to request one of our technicians to come to your home, set it up for you, and teach you exactly how to use it! They will make sure you are completely satisfied and comfortable with your new product before they leave." Here, you have not only encouraged someone to change their mind, but you have even introduced a new service to them, potentially increasing your sales, instead of driving them away.

As you can see, the power of persuasion is strong. When used correctly, you can encourage people to see things differently, and try things your way. It may seem difficult to get started at first, as new skills often are. However, the more you practice persuasion, the easier it will become for you. As you begin to master this art, you will see that it is actually incredibly easy. Persuasion has the ability to get us almost anything we want in life, which is a valuable skill when we are working on creating the lives we desire.

CHAPTER 2

MIND CONTROL

When people see the term mind control, they think one of two things: master hypnotist, or con artist. People believe that mind control is a vicious, cruel thing that has the ability to encourage people to do bad things. The reality is actually quite the opposite. The meaning of mind control is slightly blurry.

When you are using mind control, it only works if the person who you are using it on is actually being receptive. If you suggest something that firmly goes against their beliefs or desires, no matter how hard you try or how many techniques you apply, they will not respond. So, no, one could not encourage someone else to hurt someone and then have that person testify in court that they were under mind control. If they actually went out and hurt someone on their own, this was the result of their own thought waves. While it is *absolutely never* recommended that you attempt to encourage anyone to do so, it is important to realize too that unless they actually wanted to, you cannot force them to.

What mind control actually is, is the effective implementation of persuasion and NLP tactics. In essence, you use these techniques on someone who is receptive and you drive their mind in the direction they want to go. They will never know you have done this, but you will. Because of this, you are in control of their mind, technically.

Mind control is a very powerful tool that is the key driver in you being able to see the results you desire from situations you want to. If you are using your other skills properly, then the power of mind control will fall into place naturally. When this happens, you know you are succeeding in your other strategies.

Beyond the signal that your other strategies are working, the mind control portion of these techniques is actually incredibly important. When people are succumbing to your techniques, they are going to show different signs that are going to help affirm to you whether or not you are succeeding. This means that you can continue with your progress until you achieve your desired results. However, if someone shows the signs that they are not yet where you need them to be, you can adjust your strategies to increase your likelihood of having a successful interaction where you are in control over the entire situation.

Mind control is important. Without it, your entire art would be rendered ineffective. If you are going to effectively implement persuasion and NLP strategies, you should prepare to be taking over the power of being in control over your own mind, and other peoples'. By understanding this power, and appreciating its value, then using it for your own benefit, you have the ability to effectively guide people into thinking and acting in your favor.

CHAPTER 3

NLP

Neuro Linguistic Programming, or NLP for short. This method sounds like it could be a scary, scientific strategy that may be too difficult for the average person to comprehend, let alone render effective. While the specific details may be a little harder to grasp, the reality is that this incredible technique can be learned by anyone! Including you, as you read this guide book and hone your craft!

When used effectively, NLP is an excellent tool to help people in many positive ways. It is an incredible approach to use when you are communicating or working on personal development. It is even used by psychotherapists to assist people with their problems, such as PTSD from trauma, or healing addictions. This strategy is an amazing strategy that uses theory to support its effectiveness, and when used correctly, has been proven to work several times over.

NLP is a strategy that was created by two men named Richard Bandler and John Grinder. They developed this technique in the 1970s in their practices in California, USA. While there is a lot of scientific studies that suggest this technique is ineffective, this simply isn't true. Many people who use NLP in their lives will tell you that they have personally seen the effectiveness of this strategy and can attest to its ability to successfully change thoughts. Many hypnotherapists, as well as organizations and companies who use it to help changes people's lives, continue to use this method in order to create these changes.

The theory behind NLP is that there is a connection between neurological processes, language, and behavior patterns! The idea is that by changing these patterns, you can achieve certain goals you have set in your life. When people use NLP effectively, it has been reported that massive change can occur in as little as one session. Even

NEGOTIATION

though there may be no science to support these claims, the evidence of people who have experienced success after having NLP therapy is undeniably high.

When you are using NLP, there are three basic concepts that you will need to understand. These concepts include: subjectivity, consciousness, and learning. By understanding these concepts and how they affect a person's behavioral patterns, ideally you will be able to change their patterns. If you use them effectively, you should be able to change them in your favor, whatever that may be.

The first concept, subjectivity, expresses the idea that all humans experience the world in a subjective representation of their experiences. Essentially, NLP studies the exact structure of subjective experiences. What this means is that when people experience things through their subjective consciousness, they experience what they personally interpret, and sometimes not what actually is the reality. These subjective conscious experiences are developed through the five senses and language. In other words, they experience images, sounds, flavors, tactile sensations, and odors, as well as think in a natural language and all of that combines to create a specific interpretation of the present experience. Understanding how a certain person experiences these things subjectively is the first step in using NLP to alter their behaviors.

The second concept, consciousness, is one that is commonly heard, particularly by those who practice guided meditations and other similar mindfulness techniques. This concept implies that the human consciousness is divided into two separate components: the conscious mind, and the unconscious mind. The unconscious mind can also be referred to as the subconscious mind, though it is often simply referred to as the unconscious mind by NLP practitioners. Essentially the belief is that what happens in a person's subjective representation outside of the individual's direct awareness is what develops a person's "unconscious mind". So, these are thoughts and experiences you have that you may forget about or not be aware about.

NEGOTIATION

The third and final concept of NLP is learning. NLP uses a method of learning called modelling which means that you are capable of codifying and reproducing an exemplar in order to produce desired results. Ideally, you can do this in absolutely any field of activity that falls within' the exemplar's area of expertise. An important part of this codification process is using representations of sensory experiences and linguistic representations of someone's subjective of the exemplar while the expertise is being passed on to the listener.

By using all of the concepts of NLP together in this unique skill, you can increase your ability to derive your desired results in life. Using NLP is a large part of making persuasion effective, which is what ultimately leads you down the path of mind control. This way, you are capable of ultimately assisting people in arriving to your desired thought patterns and providing you with your desired results.

CHAPTER 4

EXECUTION

In order to successfully use persuasion, mind control and NLP to design your dream life, you are going to first need to understand the balance that must occur between the three. While many books specialize in one or the other, this one has been crafted to specialize in all three because this is what will ultimately make your practice most effective. Once you clearly understand this balance and how to use each skill to enhance the value you are deriving from the other ones, you will be ready to fully execute the practices of persuasion, mind control and NLP to start creating your desired life *right now*!

Balance

Creating a balance between persuasion, mind control and NLP is paramount if you are going to be successful in any of them. Some books emphasize one and include the others as mere steps in the entire practice, but the truth is that all three are equally beneficial in helping you achieve your desired goals. To understand the concept, all you need to know is that: persuasion is the technique that will guide people in your desired direction, mind control is the technique that allows you to recognize whether you are effectively producing your desired results or if you need to adjust your practice, and NLP provides you with the appropriate language and techniques to enhance the effectiveness of persuasion and increase the quality of your mind control efforts.

In order to achieve a harmonious balance, you are going to start with persuasion, infuse it with NLP strategies, and evaluate the quality of mind control being experienced at that time. Once you understand how to dance between the three techniques effectively, you will be able to guide a conversation in any direction you desire, to achieve any result you desire. As you see that mind control is being effective, you know you can further persuade someone's thoughts to change and use alternative NLP methods to deepen the effectiveness. However, if you realize at any point that mind control is not being activated efficiently, you can adjust your practice and increase your likelihood of regaining control over the situation.

Identify Your Objective

Prior to effectively implementing persuasion, mind control and NLP techniques on someone, you are going to need to identify why you are trying to do so. If you are unsure as to where you are leading a person, you are going to have a difficult time getting them there. Imagine driving a car with someone directing you who had no idea where you were going. You would end up somewhere confusing and messy, with zero returned results because the sense of direction was unclear. Before you begin using these strategies, it is paramount that you identify exactly what your objective is. Do you want to close a sale? Land a date? Change someone's opinion from a negative to a positive? Encourage your spouse to eat what *you* want for dinner, the third night in a row? Regardless of what your objective is, you need to be clear on it before you start your conversation. This way, each time you reevaluate the effectiveness of your mind control strategies, you will be able to affirm whether or not you are successfully venturing further in the direction you desire.

Questions

The first step in persuading someone is identifying where they already are in their minds so that you know exactly where you need to take them. You don't want to do this by merely asking undirected or misguided questions, however. If you are not clear in the questions you are asking, you may inadvertently drive someone in the wrong direction. Instead, you need to ask questions that are going to plant seeds to drive people in the direction you want them to go. Instead of "Do you know why you care about this?" you should say "Are you one of the people positively impacted by this experience?" this means that you are implanting the idea that there are positive impacts, and that if they are not experiencing them, there is a potential that they could be. If they are already experiencing the positive impacts, then they will feel affirmed that the situation is positive overall. The questions you ask should guide people in the direction you want to take them in the end. Doing this will allow you to use their own answers later in order to help get them there. This is actually vital, so it is important that you practice asking the right questions.

Saying "And" and "But"

Using these two words in your conversations is an important part of taking people from where they already are in their minds, and driving them to where you want them to be. They may already be the two most common words used by everyone, but this only increases the effectiveness in two ways. One: you won't have to try hard to infuse them into your conversation. Two: you are using words that are already comfortable to them, increasing your likelihood of success.

When someone uses the word "but", it usually erases the meaning of the words said up until that point. "It is free, but you have to buy warranty first" will immediately erase the idea that it is free

NEGOTIATION

because you have to pay for the warranty. As you can see, it pretty much erases the entire meaning of the words before it, not unlike white out on a page. This is one of the easiest ways to infuse your conversation with subliminal persuasion in order to achieve your desired results. You start with the bad news, throw in a "but", and end with the good news. The people are not going to think about what you have said before, because they will be focused on what you said after "but", instead. So, if you were to change the aforementioned sentence to read: "You do have to purchase the warranty to protect your product, but otherwise this item is completely free, and this is a once in a lifetime deal!" This way, the person will not focus on the fact that they do have to pay money for a warranty, because they will be focused on the fact that they are getting a product completely free! If you notice, in that sentence we used the wording "and this is a once in a lifetime deal!" which includes added benefit, further increasing the quality of your persuasion techniques. Ideally, you will continue to add extra benefits until the bad news is drown out. In the end, the person will see how great your offer is!

"Because"

The word because is a powerful word that allows you to give reason to any statement you make, which helps people reason with you, in return. In some studies, using the word "because" increases the effectiveness of a sentence by up to 93-94%! The study that exposed this was one in which there were office people who needed to use the printer. For those who merely said "Can I use the printer please?" they were asked to wait. However, if they said "Can I use the printer please, *because* I need to make some copies." Their effectiveness increased exponentially, as high as 94%. The reason this technique works so well is because our minds require that things make sense to us, especially if we are going to be required to take action. If we aren't given a reason as to why we need to take action, the likelihood is that our action will be slow to happen, if it even happens at all. As long as the reason given isn't completely ridiculous, people are going to pick it up and take it. If you are looking to get someone to spring to action, the best way is to give them a reason why. Say "because…" and give your reason, even if it's a very minimal reason, and you will see incredible differences in the amount of action taken.

A Which Means B

When you use this strategy, you are teaching people that A will mean B for them. In other words, if they do ____, it will mean ____. This might seem like an obvious use of subliminal persuasion techniques, but it's actually an incredibly important one. At a first glance, this technique might seem harder. What you're really doing, however, is persuading someone to do (A) because it will mean (B). Let's look at an example to get a clearer idea on what this means, exactly. "I agree, this item can be difficult to use at first, because you have probably never used anything like this, which means that you will be learning something new and you will receive value you never knew was possible!" In this example, we have used because, which you have already learned, we have used and, and we have constructed it into a persuasive sentence using "A, which means B." In this sentence, A was that the item is more difficult to use, and B was that the item provides value they never knew was possible.

Essentially, you are taking someone's current opinion, and reframing it to mean something positive. By giving a positive meaning to their opinion, you shift their focus to a more positive outlook which can earn you a sale, in this case. You can also use this in teaching or training, relationships, and other areas of life.

Patterns in Awareness

Recognizing patterns in awareness is an incredible technique in assisting you with wording your sentences in order to get what you are looking for. In order to master this skill, you need to understand exactly what it means. Read the following paragraph, and then learn what patterns in awareness means:

> *Everyone knows that a good TV is necessary to highlight your living room effectively. In your search for a new TV, it wouldn't surprise me if you've already realized that a good TV can be made great with the right sound system. I'm sure you know that sound systems provide a much more enjoyable experience with your new TV because it increases the quality of your*

NEGOTIATION

audio output. What type of sound system would you consider purchase with your new TV: total surround sound, or a modern and sleek sound bar?

In the above conversation, we used subliminal persuasion as an opportunity to guide someone to want to purchase a sound bar along with their new TV. We did that by first identifying that they were looking for a new TV. Then, we did not leave room for them to wonder whether or not they needed a sound system, instead we guided them to realize that a sound system was an important part of a new TV set up. If we would have simply said "would you like to purchase a new sound bar, too?" the person buying the TV would likely say "no" because they are already spending money on a new TV. However, we told them that the sound bar will make a good TV great, making them want to invest the extra couple of hundred dollars so that they can have a great experience, instead. Additionally, we provided a "because" statement, which shows that they will enjoy their experience even more because there is an increased quality in the sound of their shows. Finally, we ended with a question that did not ask "do you want a sound bar?" we said instead asked a question that asked whether they would consider a total surround sound system, or a modern and sleek sound bar. At this point, they are not thinking "yes" or "no" regarding the sound bar, instead they are thinking about which type they would want. We have slipped through the conscious mind and made it a fact that they need the sound bar, rather than allowing them to formulate a "no" opinion, and having to change that. It is easier to lay a positive foundation than it is to turn a negative reaction into a positive one.

Understanding the patterns in awareness means that you have the ability to understand how the conscious mind will think to certain sentences or questions. Then, instead of structuring your question in a way that allows the other person to become turned off and say "no", you can structure it in a way that makes them think "yes" and start to imagine what your opinion would look like in their own lives. This allows you to slip into the subconscious mind and effortlessly get your desired results from any conversation you might

NEGOTIATION

have, regardless of what your preferred outcome may be!

In order to slip facts into your conversation, there are a few words you should use. By using these words, you eliminate the questioning portion and you implant the following sentence as a fact instead of a question or suggestive statement. The following are sentence tools you can use to imply facts in your conversation:

- Obviously
- Clearly
- Undoubtedly
- As you know
- Evidently
- Everybody knows
- I'm sure you know that

Using these words are going to help you bypass questions and implant knowledge on the person listening to you. For example, if you were to say

"Do you want to buy warranty for your new computer?" people are probably going to say no. Warranty for many means hassle, it also puts a negative and unwanted idea that their perfect, shiny new computer might one day have a problem. Naturally, they reject the idea. Instead, you could say "As you know we offer a phenomenal warranty, it's $49 extra but that's minimal compared to what you may pay in the future if anything ever goes wrong, and as we know, it can be easy for mistakes to happen! This warranty is awesome because it allows us to guarantee that your new computer will be as great as new for the next five years!" This way, you don't ask about the warranty but you make its value a fact, and you erase the fee they pay by saying "but". Plus, you give them all of the details as to why the computer warranty is so valuable, which makes them much more likely to purchase it.

Agreement

People *love* to be agreed with and understood by the people they are talking to. This technique might seem incredibly obvious, but the reality is that we love to be agreed with so much that we will actually change our thoughts in order to be agreed with. Ever heard of peer pressure? This technique is a subliminal persuasion strategy that allows you to use the idea of peer pressure in reverse. Instead of you making them agree with you, you are going to agree with them, which will in turn make them agree with you! Easy, right?

When someone disagrees with you, what they are ultimately implying is that everything you said was garbage and they think you are wrong. Then, when they try and tell you what you "should" think, you don't listen because you are annoyed that they've told you that you are wrong! At this point, you shut down from the conversation and no longer listen to anything they have to say. It is likely that you may even work harder to eliminate yourself from the conversation so you no longer have to talk to them. As humans, we dislike being disagreed with or told we are wrong, it often hurts our ego and makes us unhappy with the current conversation. It puts our backs up.

Instead of telling people they are wrong, you should invest some time in learning this persuasion strategy, because the reality is that people aren't always going to agree with you. So, when they disagree with you, you need to be prepared to find a way to have them in agreeance again so you can have your desired outcome! This strategy allows you to do exactly that. At no point will you be telling someone they're wrong, or getting their backs up and having them ignore you from there on out. Instead, they will be happy because you agree with them and they will continue to agree with you in return!

In order to use this technique, instead of saying "no, actually…" you should say "I agree, and…". What this does is shows the other person that you agree, and then provides them another piece of information so that they can agree with you. You elaborate off of their point to draw the conversation back in your favor. For example, let's say you were in a relationship with someone and they felt as though you were not connecting as much as you used to. Perhaps they say to you "We don't go out together anymore!" you could say "I agree, it has been a long time since we have gone out together. And, this means that you are even more important

NEGOTIATION

to me because I am willing to sacrifice our time together now so that we can have an incredible future together, with plenty of time to enjoy each other's company as much as we desire!" This allows you to agree with the person talking to you, keep them on your side, and open up the conversation while you make your point. Instead of disagreeing with them or getting their back up and potentially causing an argument, you get them in agreeance with you and the conversation ends in your favor.

Some people may have a hard time with this one, because you won't always agree with what the other person is saying. After all, that's why you're currently in a predicament with a disagreement, is it not? It is natural for people not to agree with each other all of the time. When you say "I agree, and..." you are not lying to the other person. Just because you say that you agree doesn't necessarily mean that you feel the exact same way as they do. Instead, it means that you agree either about a certain part of what they have said, or that you agree in their opinion but not what it contains.

Pacing and Leading

The process of pacing and leading works by you pacing their present experience and leading them into the experience you want them to have. So, you will use descriptions to describe the current situation, and then you will lead them with a final statement. This can be done in many ways, but will always involve a couple of sentences outlining the situation and then essentially calling them to action. Let's imagine you're managing a business and you want to promote someone, but first they need to show a few extra talents in order to prove they're ready for the promotion. If you want to encourage them to work for that promotion, you could say "Clearly, you work is consistently of high quality, you meet your deadlines on time, and you are prepared to further your career with our company. Because of these reasons, I am sure you are prepared to take on extra duties to get yourself that promotion." In this situation, you outline where the current situation lies: they have high quality work, meet deadlines on time, and want to further their career. That is why they are ready to take on some extra tasks, so that they can get the promotion.

NEGOTIATION

Anchoring

Anchoring is an NLP technique that has a strong ability to encourage someone to agree with you or act in your favor. In order to anchor effectively, you first have to understand what it means. To anchor is essentially to instill in another person's subconscious that a certain part of your body is "good" and another part is "bad". So, when you are saying something negative or uncomfortable, you will point to the "bad" area. When you are saying something good, or exciting, you will point to the "good" area. This way, you will be able to access the visual sensations of a person and increase your power through this NLP technique.

To start anchoring, what you are going to do is pick two areas on your body: for example, let's imagine the right side is "bad" and the left side is "good". Every time you say something that is bad or elicits ill feelings, you are going to subtly point or gesture to the "bad" side. Then, when you say things that spark good or positive feelings, you will gesture to the "good" side. You want to do this from the get go, so that when you are ready to really guide the conversation to home plate, you can use the good side to encourage the person further. So, let's say your end goal is to receive a promotion from your boss. You have associated the left side of your body with positivity. When you finally come to the part of the conversation where you ask for the raise, you could say "so, can I have a raise?" and you will gesture to the left side of your body once again. This will encourage your boss to say "yes" because they see it will be a good thing.

Sensory Words

A great way to really get into someone's subconscious is to use sensory words. This is going to allow their mind to do something without you directly asking them to do it. This technique is a great way to subliminally drive someone to think about a certain subject that you would like them to think about. For example, let's say you want your spouse to remember when you first got together, as a means to rekindle the spark. Instead of saying "Do you remember when we first started dating? We had so much spark. I miss that." Which may cause them to feel bad about themselves, wondering why they aren't capable of providing the spark anymore, you can instead say "Can you

NEGOTIATION

imagine how different life was when we met? I still love the way you make me feel." This will drive them to visualize those times when the spark was brighter, and will also imply the sensation of feel, which will have them thinking about how it really felt when you were in your honeymoon stages in your relationship. This will help them feel more confident in their ability to make you feel great and will likely encourage them to want to have those same fiery feelings again. Especially if you pair this sentence with other persuasion techniques!

You can also instill these words in a more subliminal way. For example, instead of simply saying "imagine you are in your work office with a stack of papers on your desk and the boss breathing down your neck" you can say "imagine a stressful time when you're working really hard and..." which will have them naturally thinking about that without you physically putting the image in their mind. It is important that you get their imagination working for you, by making the images you want it to make without you directly asking them to picture what you want them to think about. The better you can do this, the easier your mind control strategies will be! You should do this with all of the senses: sight ("imagine", "you see", "clearly", etc.), sound ("hear", "listen", "it sounds like", etc.), touch ("it feels like", "I feel", etc.), taste ("that's a bitter thing to say", "how sweet", etc.). The more senses you can infuse in the conversation, the more invested they will be and the more control you will have over them.

Recap

By now, you are probably feeling confident in the different ideas you've learned, and are ready to go use them in real life. Ideally, you are going to want to start with only a couple at a time, as this will allow you the opportunity to really become fluent in using them. If you try and use too many at once, you may become overwhelmed or confused, and your conversation could become awkward and potentially retrieve you the opposite of your desired results. The more you practice, the stronger and more fluent you will become with persuasion techniques and the greater your results will be. As you feel more confident in your ability to use and get results from these techniques, you can

NEGOTIATION

implement more and more until you are a swift talker getting your way in virtually any situation.

CHAPTER 5

Examples

Understanding the various techniques is important, however it can sometimes be hard to understand exactly how these techniques can be used in real life situations. In the previous chapter, you learned details on how you can use these techniques, but the intention of this book is to have you feeling extremely comfortable in your practice of persuasion, mind control and NLP.

Let's explore exactly how you can use these strategies in real-life situations. You are going to discover exactly how you can structure sentences in order to guide the conversation depending on what results you desire. Persuasion, mind control and NLP works incredibly well in various areas of life, which means that you can use it in virtually any conversation. In fact, the more you practice using it, the easier it is going to become and the more naturally it will be for you.

Persuasion, mind control and NLP is an excellent tool for creating your entire life, from work to relationships, and even in your own mind. As you become more skilled, you can start to address your own mind as well, and control your own thoughts and emotions in order to create the internal reality you desire, as well.

Sales

Using persuasion in sales is an excellent way to increase your sales numbers and generally increase your profitability. Whether you run your own business, are paid commissions, or are looking for a promotion or raise, working your sales is a great way to do it. Luckily, persuasion, mind control and NLP are some of the best opportunities to increase your sales quotas! Look at some of the common sales situations and find some effective answers that assist finalizing sales!

Scenario One: Warranty (Sensory)

Sales person: "Would you like to purchase warranty?"

Customer: "No thanks"

End conversation.

Instead, you could say *"For only $49, you can have your product guarantee for three years. Imagine how good it will feel, knowing that you're in safe hands in case any of one of those several components inside of your machine burns out!"*

Scenario Two: Warranty (Reason)

Sales person: "Would you like to protect your machine with warranty for just $49 extra?"

Customer: "No thank you"

End conversation.

Instead, you could say *"We offer an incredible warranty that is an extra $49, but it provides you with three years-worth of protection in the event anything goes wrong, and you can be sure that you will only be* *dealing with experts. And, you get a free consultation to learn to use your new product!"*

Scenario Three: Selling (Laying the Foundation)

Sales Person: "I see you are looking at a TV, would you like a bigger (more expensive) one?"

Customer: "No thanks, these ones are big enough."

Instead, you could say *"I see you are looking at a TV! What a great choice, purchasing new technology is always so much fun. I wouldn't be surprised if you have already browsed our selection of 4K TVs that provide optimal viewing experience. The value of those TVs are incredible, when you consider the quality you are receiving and how modern the technology is! And, they even come with an impressive new program that allows you to effortlessly search and navigate channels from your smart phone!"*

Scenario Four: Selling (Add-On's)

Sales Person: "Would you like one of our technicians to come help you set it up?"

Customer: "No thank you."

Instead, you could say: *"I see you have purchased a new computer! New technology is so much fun, especially learning how to use all of the different components effectively. We have incredible technicians who are trained to help you learn exactly how you can use every component of your new computer to optimize your experience and increase your computer's ability to serve your needs! It costs an additional $99 for the set up service, but it is really important if you desire to get the most use out of your new computer. And, they even help customize the entire set up to your specific needs. Did you know you can even sync your computer with your phone to automatically share pictures you take? When would you like to schedule your set up?"*

Scenario Five: Selling (Resistance)

Sales person: "Are you interested in that new patio set?"

Customer: "It's too expensive for me."

Instead, you could say: *"I agree, it is an expensive patio set, but that allows us to ensure that you are getting the highest quality there is! Did you know this patio set is made of real wood, and it features a finish that protects it from various weather conditions? And, it comes with an umbrella to keep you protected from the sun!"*

Work

Using persuasion, mind control and NLP in your work space is a great way to increase how enjoyable your job is. You can use these techniques to help you get a better position, increase your pay, or even make your work conditions more desirable. In fact, you can even use them to help you land a job!

Scenario One: Job Interview

Many people enter a job interview with the idea to request information on what the job will get for *them*. Instead of entering the interview with the intention of answering questions, enter with the intention of asking some. Asking appropriate questions will help the employer imagine you in the position already, and that will increase their likelihood of hiring you: especially if they like what they are imagining. Let's review some interview questions you should *avoid* first.

- *"How much money does the position pay?"*

- *"How many vacation and sick days do your employees get?"*

- *"What exactly does your company do?"*

These questions show that you are ill informed and that you are not interested in giving your all when you work with the company. Questions along these lines give the idea that you are lazy and might be an employee who is looking to get paid for doing the bare minimum. Employers avoid these types of employee, as they damage the work morale, productivity, and other important elements of running a successful business. If you want to get hired by someone, or at least be offered several positions if you are shopping around for a new job, you need to ask questions that are providing the employers with value. This will enable you to show them that you are curious about how you can help them, and in return they will want to help you, too. Asking these questions may even help you get hired at a higher pay rate, since you are adding more value to their company. Questions you should ask include:

- "What is the company's preferred management style?"

- "When I start work, who will I report to?"

- "Imagine I was to be hired, how would my daily duties look?"

- "When is the next time I will hear from you?"

- "What training opportunities do you offer?"

- "Are there opportunities for promotions in the future?"

- "How do you measure and review performance levels?"

Scenario Two: Asking for A Raise or Promotion

Instead of flat out asking for a promotion or a raise and potentially being denied, you need to offer valuable reasons as to why you deserve a promotion or a raise. Employers want to know that they are allocating their money effectively, and while they are willing to pay their employees what they value them at, it is also important that they aren't *over* paying their employees. While asking for a raise may allow your employer to know you want one, it will not set the tone for you to actually receive one in the near future. What you need to do is use subliminal persuasion to allow them to see how valuable you are as an employee, which will help encourage them to hire you.

Something you might say would be:

"Hello Mr. Will, I am looking to receive an increase in my responsibilities. I feel that I deserve a promotion, but I know that promotions are only offered to those who are valuable. Because of that, I realize that you will want to see how valuable I am to your company, and truly get a grasp on how much benefit I add to your team. And, I know that promotions come with added responsibility, and I am prepared to show you that I can handle that."

This allows your employer to know you're looking for a promotion and a raise, but you aren't just looking for a free hand-out. You know you are valuable, and you are willing to increase your value for the company in return for that promotion and raise.

NEGOTIATION

Managing

These techniques are an incredible opportunity to increase the quality of your management skills in order to see greater return from your employees. When you use persuasion, mind control and NLP, you can encourage your employees to do more work, be more productive, and offer more value to the company. All of these will ultimately increase your value to the company as a manager, or increase your company's overall profitability and productivity if you are the owner.

Scenario One: Increasing Productivity

Increasing productivity from your employees requires that you are able to communicate with your employees and understand where they are coming from. The more you can encourage their productivity to sky rocket, the better your company will do. Imagine you are in a team meeting, and you ask your employees *"what is one thing that could increase our productivity?"* in return, an employee says *"make our tasks more attainable!"* You could say *"I agree our goals sometimes seem as though they are hard to achieve. However, I know that you are an incredible team with so much value to offer. That is why we hired you! I know you have what it takes to help us reach these levels. And, I know you will be able to do them effortlessly, too!"*

Scenario Two: Motivating Employees

Motivating individual employees can be hard sometimes. Occasionally, employees become burnt out from their responsibilities and it can cause them to become uninspired in their work. In order to re-ignite their inspiration, you can use persuasion, mind control and NLP to achieve this!

Imagine you are working the morning shift and an employee shoes up and feels unmotivated to work. You could say *"Get to work!"* which the employee would likely shrug off or potentially even get annoyed by. Or, you could say *"Listen, Tom! You are an incredible part of this team and I really appreciate all of the value you add to our company. Because of all of the hard work you do, we have been able to make our goals this week, and even for the entire month. And, I think you can help us go even further! What do you say?"*

Scenario Three: Team Motivation

NEGOTIATION

Occasionally, you may notice that your entire team is feeling unmotivated or uninspired. In workplaces, sometimes if one or two people are in this mindset, the feeling can spread like a wild fire and before you know it your entire team isn't as motivated as they once were! As a manager, it is your duty to make sure that they are feeling motivated and inspired to get their jobs done, and do them well. Instead of saying *"Listen team, we have really failed to make our targets this quarter, I need you to step up your game!"* You could say *"I agree it has been a hard quarter this time. Sales have been low, and our targets aren't being met as effortlessly as we generally do. But, I believe this quarter we can re-claim our strengths and smash our targets! And, I know you are just the people for the job, and I look forward to assisting you in meeting your sales targets!"*

Relationships

Relationships can be hard. Whether you are friends, new lovers, or in a long term relationship, there can come times where it can be hard to get what you want. Especially when that requires you to take a person from where they may currently be in their minds, and leading them to a new spot that benefits you better! Realistically, it will also benefit them better. If you want to learn to use persuasion, mind control and NLP in your relationships, try these techniques.

Scenario One: Dating

When you are dating, it can be really hard to understand where exactly your date is, mentally. Sometimes, you don't know if they're thinking about seeing you again or not. For this reason, you don't just want to ask *"so, will I see you again?"* because that leaves you wide open for a big fat "nope!" Unless you are very clear that they *do* in fact want to see you again!

Instead of worrying about rejection, you can use these strategies to see someone for a second date, you could say things such as:

"I wonder if you also feel how deep of a connection we appear to share, and how meaningful that truly is because everyone knows the internet can be a tough place to meet someone so amazing."

NEGOTIATION

"I agree, spending time together has been so much fun. I would love to see you again, because I really feel like we connect well and your company has been so enjoyable for me!"

Scenario Two: Conflict Resolution

It happens. We all get into a situation where conflicts occur. The easiest way to manage conflict in your relationship is with an "I agree" statement. As you know, people *love* to be agreed with. When you agree with someone, even if you are leading them from their position to your own, you are much more likely to gain traction and effectively lead them in your desired direction. The following are some examples of how you might use persuasion for conflict resolution in relationships.

Spouse: "You shouldn't have done that."

You: "I agree, I made a mistake and it was wrong of me. But, I hope you understand I made it with the best of intentions, and I only had your highest good in mind when I was doing it."

Friend: "We never see each other anymore."

You: "I agree our time together has been limited these days. But, I really feel that it makes the time we do spend together more enjoyable, and it makes me value your friendship so much more."

Child: "I never get my way."

You: "I agree we don't always get our way. But, that doesn't mean you never get to do what you want and I am sure you will remember that is true. I know you understand that I am only saying no because it is for your benefit."

Spouse: "You work too much."

You: "I agree I work a lot. But, I work a lot because I want to make sure that you are able to enjoy all life has to offer. And, I am preparing us so that we can spend much more time together in the future."

Negotiating

Occasionally there will come times in life where you are going to need to have strong negotiating skills. As you might guess, negotiating effectively is one of the times that persuasion techniques are most effective and beneficial! There are many

NEGOTIATION

reasons why you might need to negotiate, so you will want to take what you learn here and improvise for your unique situation.

Scenario One: Getting Your Way

Imagine you are preparing to purchase a car, but the car you desire is about $5000 too expensive for your budget. Instead of walking away, you could use persuasion techniques to reduce the cost of the car!

Sales Person: "This car is valuated at $25,000 and we are selling it for just $22,500! It is a smoking deal!"

You: "I agree, that is an incredible deal! But, I am offering you a trade in valued at $9,000, and I would like to see that price come down a bit more. And, I intend to offer you additional service in the future."

Sales Person: "With your trade in valued at $9,000, you can have this car for just $13,500 out of your pocket! That is an incredible opportunity!"

You: "I agree it certainly is an incredible deal. My trade in is a high quality, top of the line model, and I would like to see it at least $16,000 for it. And, I know it is *worth this value because I have kept it in immaculate condition. It even has its original floor mats, and they're still clean as new!"*

Sales Person: "I can't offer you $16,000 for your trade in, but I can offer you $12,000."

You: "I feel that you can come a bit higher, but I appreciate you are willing to meet me in the middle. If you are willing to give me $14,000 for my vehicle, I will be happy to purchase my new car and the warranty on it! And, I will recommend all of my friends come here to purchase their cars through you!"

Sales Person: "Deal!"

In the above conversation, you have agreed that the sales person cannot give you an excessive amount for your trade-in car, but you have also brought the price up by $5,000. Since the sales person has not already covered the topic of warranty, they are unaware that you were already willing to purchase warranty on your vehicle. So, you have increase the value of your offer to them, without increasing what you expected to pay yourself. Instead, you earned yourself a sweet deal!

CHAPTER 6

TROUBLESHOOTING

Persuasion, mind control and NLP sound so easy. You practice some incredible strategies, you implement them, and bam you are getting your way all the time! But, what about when that isn't happening? You are using your techniques and you aren't seeking the results you desire. From time to time, this is going to happen. However, it should not be happening every single time. In fact, more often than not, you should actually be seeing a positive return from your efforts. If you aren't, there are some things you can consider to help you increase your success with persuasion, mind control, and NLP.

Identify The Problem

Sometimes, it can be incredible easy to identify exactly where a situation is going wrong. Others, it can be a little harder. It is important, however, to understand when your efforts are starting to fail so that you can really understand where you need to improve your game. Generally, in order to troubleshoot you must first identify the trouble. If you can already recall the exact moment that your conversations start to swing out of your control, then you will have an easier time learning *why* that is happening. However, if you are totally stumped, there is something you can do to get clear on what is going wrong. In order to get this clarity, simply recall a recent conversation you had where you attempted to use persuasion and it failed. Take note of the exact moment resistance started. Sometimes, you will discover that resistance started long before they verbalized their resistance. You might see their arms cross, their feet start pointing to the exit, their eyes looking away frequently, fidgeting, or other signs of discomfort. All of these signs show that the recipient was not being affected positively by your efforts. Once you understand the exact moment that the person has developed a sense of resistance, recall exactly what you were saying immediately before that happened. Try and identify what about the sentence could possibly make someone feel closed off or put their back up. Did you use your wording wrong? Was your "because" reasoning not strong enough? Did you make the "bad news" sound excessively bad? Were you already off course and continued pushing for something they did not want, without agreeing and understanding their position? It is important that you know exactly what the issue was so that you can fix it in a future conversation and prevent it from happening again. Sometimes, a simple review of your technique with a subsequent adjustment to your style is all you need to make a conversation more effective!

Slow Down

Occasionally, people will become incredibly excited about their newfound persuasion skills and will want to use them all right away. This can lead to a few different scenarios, neither of which will play out well in your favor. One scenario might be that you are too excited and you fail to use them fluently, and therefore it becomes obvious that you are attempting to guide someone's opinion in a different direction. Once they sense this, they will be put off of what you have to say and will not want to listen to you. Other times, you may try too hard to remember all of the techniques and therefore your sentences will sound awkward and uncomfortable. Once again, your recipient will have a harder time agreeing with you or coming to your desired frame of mind because they will not feel comfortable in what you are saying. If you are not comfortable, neither is the person you are talking to. In those situations, the recipient will either develop an understanding of the fact that you are attempting or persuade them, or they will feel awkward and want to end the conversation as quickly as possible, meaning you will not have the outcome in your favor.

Take your time, and truly practice one or two strategies at a time. You don't necessarily have to spend weeks perfecting each one, but the more time you genuinely invest in getting better, the easier it is going to be to learn the entire language. Essentially, the more time you give yourself to learn the art of persuasion, the quicker you are going to actually learn it. It is easiest to start with small things, such as using "and" "but" and "because" in your sentences to help draw people in your desired direction. Then, you can start using patterns of awareness, "I agree" phrases, and more in order to perfect your art and optimize your results. Take your time and focus on what actually works for you, and do your best to replicate those things in future situations!

Build Your Confidence

People are naturally going to feel uncomfortable around someone who is under confident. They are either going to take advantage of you, or they are going to avoid having a conversation with you. Ultimately, you don't want either of these things to happen. Often, we lack confidence when we are not feeling well versed in our new skills. If you take your time, as previously mentioned, and give yourself space to learn the skills, you will have an easier time building your confidence in your skills.

There are also other ways you can increase your confidence and improve your persuasive abilities. You can spend time practicing new techniques on people who you are more comfortable around, such as friends and family. As you become more confident in your ability, you can move up to harder subjects, such as coworkers and your boss, and continue moving up until you can use the technique on anyone. Or, you can start with small intentions. For example, instead of walking up to a car salesman and asking for $10,000 off the asking price, you can ask for $3,000 off. Or, instead of asking a computer salesman for a $200 discount, you can ask for a free warranty. You might even start as small as persuading your spouse to take you on a date or to cook your dinner. Start with whatever you are comfortable with, and work your way up. That way, when you get to the important things, such as asking for a promotion, or landing a major sale, you are well versed, prepared and confident!

Confidence is a key component in building rapport, which is absolutely necessary if you are going to succeed in persuasion. If people are not comfortable around you, or do not feel that they can trust you, they are not going to agree with you no matter what strategies you use.

NEGOTIATION

Mind Your Intentions

Although I presume your intentions are positive or innocent, it is important to make sure that they certainly are. Sometimes, we might feel under confident or uncomfortable because we feel that our intentions are not justified or that they may present something bad for someone else. For example, we may want to make a sale but we feel bad because we don't want to cost our customer a lot of money. The reality is, if your customer is there to shop, they are prepared to spend money and they are relying on you to provide them with the highest value for their money. Instead of feeling awkward, getting them into a cheap and unreliable set up, or otherwise breaking their trust or confidence in you, you should be aware of your intentions and stick to them. As long as your intentions are benefiting *everyone* and you can understand why they are, you will be able to encourage the other person to understand how your intentions will benefit them. The more people your intentions can benefit, the better. That will make it easier for you to feel confident in your request, and it will make your recipient feel more confident in their compliance.

Accept Defeat

Occasionally you are going to be using persuasion techniques on someone and they absolutely won't work. No matter how much rapport you establish, no matter how confident you feel, and no matter how smoothly you execute your skills, you might find that sometimes you will still experience complete, unwavering resistance. The reality is that most people are going to have a positive response to your skills and attempts, but not everyone is going to submit to your requests and give you want you want.

If you are experiencing complete resistance there are two things you can do: slow completely down and plant seeds, or accept defeat. If you are not prepared to accept total defeat, you can go even slower than attempting to get all you desire from one conversation. Instead, you can plant seeds and draw it out over a few, each time slowly drawing the recipient closer and closer to your desired outcome. You can take your time, consistently

NEGOTIATION

leading them to the conclusion you want them to have, without never fully revealing your desires of what you want. This is a good idea if you are speaking with someone who is giving you incredibly high levels of resistance. Instead of revealing what you are asking for, you can simply use your strategies to guide them closer and closer to these ideas all on their own. Eventually, when you feel that you are no longer receiving high levels of resistance, you can take the conversation and drive it completely home, subliminally implanting your exact request in such a way that they simply can't deny you.

The truth is, absolute defeat does not happen. It may take several conversations, even over the duration of months to receive your desired answer, however that does not mean you will never receive it. It simply means you need to slow down, take your time, and encourage them to eventually come to your desired conclusion.

The only time you will admit complete defeat is if you personally no longer feel it is valuable for you to pursue said person. For example, perhaps you are looking to pursue someone for a sale, but you realize that it may take many months for them to agree. You know the sale would be nice, but the reality is that there are many more sales to come and it is not worth your time to invest terribly much into said sale. You can either take your time and not invest too much energy into them but still gently push them in your desired direction. Or, you can admit defeat and invest your energy in someone else who is much more likely to purchase your product.

Recap

When you are practicing your persuasion techniques and finding that you are not receiving the results you desire, the answer is often simple. You simply have to discover why you are not receiving your desired results. Then, you can slow down, build your confidence, practice your skills a little more, and try again. More often than not, the issue is rather simple and you can easily pinpoint where you have gone wrong and what you need to do in order to fix the situation. Many times, you can even approach the same person again and attempt your efforts once again and receive your desired results. Remember, it can take time, so go easy on yourself and have fun with it! The more comfortable you are with your practice, the more fluent you will become and the easier it will be for you to achieve success in the art of persuasion.

CONCLUSION

Using the art of persuasion, you can achieve any result you desire and make it seem effortless. While obstacles may arise in your path, you will have all of the tools you need in order to easily overcome those obstacles and successfully reach your goals. You can use persuasion as an effective method to allow you to request a promotion, increase rapport with your spouse, or even encourage someone to see things from your point of view. The opportunities are endless when you become fluent in persuasion, mind control, and NLP. You now have all of the tools you need to get started and become a master in the art that is your birthright.

The next step after reading this book is to take some of the easier strategies and start practicing them in your own life. Remember, it is easiest if you use these strategies on people you are already comfortable with, first. Then, you can start using them on everyone else as well, which will further help you increase your skill and convert your conversations into positive results that always land in your favor. Using your natural power of persuasion, you possess the ability to achieve any outcome you desire, and so you should feel confident in doing so.

Remember, you can use persuasion, mind control and NLP in order to achieve effective results in any area of your life. You can even use these skills to recognize your own thought patterns and alter them to be more effective and to align with your desired lifestyle! The more you practice, the easier it will become. Take your time, increase your skill, and watch your success rise!

Thank you again for choosing *"Persuasion:* The Complete Step by Step Guide on Persuasion, Mind Control and NLP." I hope this book exceeded your expectations and that you fill confident in your ability to master the art of persuasion. If you found this book useful in anyway, please give this book a positive review on Amazon, it will be much appreciated. Having a positive review from you will help this book reach many more people, so that they can benefit from the information shared within this book as well.

Once again, don't forget to grab a copy of your FREE BONUS book *"The Secrets Behind Subtle Psychology: Secrets To Getting All You Want"*. If you are interested in learning more about human psychology and being more effective in conversations, then this book is for you.

Just click here http://bit.ly/subtlepsychology

Also, If you would like to learn more about my other works, take a look at *"Persuasion: The Definitive Guide to Understanding Influence, Mind Control and NLP"* Which is the first installment in the Persuasion series where I covered the basics of persuasion and how it worked. And *"Persuasion Mastery: How to Master Persuasion, Mind Control and NLP"* Which is the second installment in the Persuasion Series where you will find advanced tips and strategies that will really take your persuasion skills to the next level. Both are easily found on the Amazon store!

NEGOTIATION

Best wishes in your successful persuasion practices!

Manipulation:

The Complete Step-by-Step Guide on Manipulation, Mind Control, and NLP

INTRODUCTION

Congratulations on purchasing your personal copy of *Manipulation: The Complete Step-by-Step Guide on Manipulation, Mind Control, and NLP*. Thank you for doing so.

The following chapters will discuss some of the many ways you can manipulate the thoughts, beliefs, and behaviors of others and how you can recognize when that same manipulation is happening to you.

You will discover how important our step-by-step guide is to identifying manipulative strategies and techniques that are being used to persuade you to do another's wished, and how quickly you can turn the tables and apply those same steps to achieve your desired outcome.

The final chapter will explore what you consider to be an active and fruitful way to use these steps. You are in control; the decision is yours. Will you use our step-by-step guide to help yourself and others toward a positive outcome? Or, will you choose to practice the darker side of manipulation and mind control?

There are plenty of books on this subject on the market; thanks again for choosing this one! Every effort was made to ensure it is full of as much useful information as possible. Please enjoy!

CHAPTER 1

Manipulating the Mind through NLP

Before we discuss the positives and negatives of manipulation through NLP, let's define the term, shall we? NLP stands for Neuro-Linguistic Programming. I'm sure that definition holds no meaning for most of you, so we'll explain it a bit further. The three words in the term NLP all represent elements that contribute to how our bodies function, what makes us think as we do, and how we form our perceptions. Ultimately, we think, believe, and behave based on those three things, and those things create our reality. This school of thought promotes the idea that there is no actual reality, only that which an individual creates through his or her NLP. Let's break down the term a bit more.

Neuro

This element oversees our bodily functions and reactions.

Linguistic

This element determines how we communicate with ourselves and others.

Programming

This feature combines our past experiences and relates it to our immediate perceptions to determine our future behaviors, which become our new reality.

The step-by-step guide on manipulation we will be discussing throughout this book is not meant to be used as a negative tool to forcefully control others, although it can. Instead, we offer these five steps to help you identify when you are being manipulated and, ways that you can persuade others to your way of thinking if it is in their best interest. When you have the other person's well-being as your primary motivation, using these five steps will help you lead them to a more positive outcome. However, if your motives are selfish, practicing these measures will only serve to frustrate you and create distrust in those you are trying to persuade.

As you read through these chapters, it may be the first time you've ever thought of manipulation in a positive light, so let's give you some examples of the power of manipulation and how to use it to benefit others and help you get your desires as well.

The Awesome Power of Manipulation

There is a theory out there that most of us experience manipulation every day, and that our freedom of choice has been slowly taken away by societal programming that has gradually changed our perception of reality. Okay, let me put that in English. For example, for years we have heard that diet products are healthy, right? We diligently read the labels to see how many calories they contain, and how much fat, carbohydrates, and sugar we will be consuming. Everything looks in line, and so we begin substituting a diet bar or a protein shake for a meal. Have you ever wondered why we eat and drink so many low-calorie products and yet millions still suffer from obesity? Isn't it odd that you rarely see a thin person eating or drinking diet products?

Why do you suppose that is? Could it be that our perceptions about diet products need to change? Perhaps—just perhaps—diet products aren't that good for us, and the ingredients they contain have changed our bodily functions along with our mistaken reality that if we consume diet products, we'll lose weight? How can this be? After all, manufacturers have told us they are low-cal and sugar-free, and they featured all those thin people in their ads and television commercials.

Television commercials, ad campaigns, and friends and family members have repeatedly told us how healthy the diet products are, and the more we heard it, the more we believed it. So, not only did our bodily functions change but so did our perceptions and behaviors, which gave us a new reality—those diet products were healthy and would make us lose weight. That's the danger of negative manipulation; it can be so strong that it changes our entire belief system. When we allow another to alter our thinking, it can take a long time to return to our previous reality. That's the awesome power of manipulation. You have the power to change another's reality.

Is It Ever Right to Manipulate Another?

Absolutely! It's right to manipulate them when you have their best interest in mind. For example, if the one you love is slowly killing themselves with drugs and you know they need to stop, it's perfectly acceptable to use your power of manipulation to intervene and empower them to create a new positive reality. If you are on a team with co-workers who cannot agree on a future vision for the project and so nothing is getting done, you are well within your rights to practice a bit of sound manipulation. Everyone is better off if it helps the team get focused on the goal.

Practicing Manipulation Has Consequences and Obligations

Once you have learned how to manipulate others, you have a duty to only use that power in a positive way. If you decide to selfishly apply the skills you will learn in these five steps, there could be significant consequences that will negatively impact your life. Once you have manipulated a person's reality, you have an obligation to mentor and guide them as they explore and investigate their new perceptions and beliefs.

The bigger the changes in perceptions and behaviors, the more support will be needed. You are not using this NLP power of manipulation correctly if you persuade someone to move in a different direction and then abandon them when they need you the most. So, along with the powers of manipulation, you owe it to yourself and others to offer guidance and encouragement along the way. Should you unintentionally lead another on a negative path, then together you must set a new desired outcome and work with one another to achieve that desired result.

Some Are Easy to Manipulate--Some Are Not
You would think those who are easy to manipulate are always the ones who are meek and introverted, but this is not always the case. Often, the very

people who think others could never manipulate them, are the easiest to influence and persuade. The seemingly stronger personalities are unsuspecting and unprepared. Because few people ever try to control those with more powerful personalities, they don't see the manipulative signals. Whereas, weaker people who experience manipulation frequently will recognize your attempts and might have built up more resistance.

It's important to remember that all of us experience manipulation every day. When you learn the five steps presented in our book, you'll quickly recognize when it's happening to you. Don't be surprised if you think you're manipulating a person when he or she is manipulating you. You see this frequently going on in close relationships, especially if one is a giver and the other a taker. The "giver" will give a little, and then a bit more — asking nothing in return, at first. The taker will enjoy the taking, and might even consider the fact that being in this relationship requires nothing of him or her. Ah, but not so fast!

Once the giver has obligated the "taker" by always being the one to give on the little things, there is a huge request made. The taker in the relationship now feels he or she has no choice but to comply after all the giver so rarely expects anything of them. Guess what? The taker, whom you would have thought was the manipulator, has now been manipulated.

What matters more than the personality type of person experiencing the manipulation is his or her motivation to change, desired outcome, and the strength of their previous programming. Some weak people play the victim, and the challenge to manipulate their thinking is almost insurmountable. Why? Because many individuals who act as victims are the ones who are manipulating you, and it's much harder to manipulate a manipulator.

Even though it would be more positive for them to get what they want by being empowered and encouraged to do so in a positive way, the victim is often too content in their role to transition to a place of power easily. They have created their reality, and

NEGOTIATION

that reality has made them a victim. We see this with people who have repeatedly been abused, beaten down, or experience constant drama. Manipulating them can be impossible because they are already getting their desired outcome. You'll understand more about this in a later chapter.

The five steps in this book will give you a roadmap of strategies and techniques that teach you to manipulate and persuade others to do what is best for them. The beauty of positive manipulation is that while helping others, you also help yourself. That's the way our world works. Some people call it Karma, but it is positive thoughts and actions attracting more positives. The same is true with negative manipulation; it draws more negative into your life and the lives of others, and so your reality will be one of loneliness and isolation when you selfishly manipulate others. After being manipulated by you for selfish gain, people won't want to be around you; you now have destroyed their trust. Coming back from that position is a long haul and one in which many never return to their former self.

What's the Difference Between Control and Manipulation?

The difference between the two is subtle, but there is a slight distinction. When you are attempting to control people, you make a suggestion to try to influence them, or out-and-out dictate to them what they will do because you have control. When you manipulate people, you arrange for them to share your experiences, and move them toward the behavior or belief that you wish them to have. You're not controlling them; you're demonstrating and explaining what is best for them, and doing so in a way that is more covert. It's that secret thing that makes all the difference. Many people can be manipulated but not controlled.

Individuals who are not good at manipulation don't achieve success because they are too outwardly controlling, and people resent that action. If used negatively, to hurt people, manipulation can be much more dangerous and lasting. The time factor is another difference between the two. When you control another's behavior, if you are no longer present to influence them constantly, it is hard to maintain that same control. Whereas, if you are manipulating people, they don't realize they are intentionally moved to think, behave, and believe in a particular manner. Because manipulation entirely changes one's perspective, they do not return to their old way of thinking as easily because you have helped them to create for themselves a new reality.

How Can You Tell When You Are Negatively Manipulated?

Don't waste your time trying to figure out IF you are experiencing manipulation—we are all shaped and managed to one extent or another. What you need to be aware of are the times' someone is trying to negatively manipulate you—to persuade or move you to do things that go against your personal values and boundaries. Here are ten ways to identify when you are the victim of negative manipulation.

1. 1.Although you have changed your beliefs and behaviors, you have an underlying unrest about the new you.

2. You are obsessed with your new reality and talk about it all the time as if to justify why you believe and behave the way you do. However, when you try to describe why you think and act this way now, your explanations are weak and unsatisfying. You end up saying "Well, it's hard to explain," to others.

3. 3.You often feel anxious, distrusting, jealous, or incompetent around your manipulator, especially if that person is someone with whom you are involved with romantically.

4. You have extreme mood swings, and your happiness is dependent upon the attitude of your manipulator.

5. You hold your manipulator in such high regard and feel as though you are betraying him or her if you should dare to disagree.

6. 6.You have a lower self-esteem unless your manipulator is there to boost your spirit.

NEGOTIATION

7. 7.You are more guarded in your words and actions. You do this because manipulators frequently withdraw their friendship or affections from you when you have said or done something that is contrary to what they believe or how they behave.

8. 8.It seems like you can never do anything right, and you find yourself apologizing all the time.

9. Your primary purpose is to make your manipulator happy, and you find yourself sacrificing your happiness for his or hers.

10. You become more isolated from your former friends and find that your social life is almost non-existent except for that of your manipulator.

Although these feelings and behaviors would only happen in the most extreme cases, you might experience several at once in a new friendship or relationship. It never hurts to keep your eyes and ears open to the fact that manipulation occurs all around us. Some of it is an attempt to persuade us to a different reality that is so much better than that in which we leave behind. However, some manipulators are only out for what will benefit themselves, and it matters not who gets caught in the crossfire. If they can use you to get what they want, you become the next rung on their ladder to success.

If you should recognize some of these ten signs that indicate negative manipulation, challenge your manipulator and observe his or her response. Standing up for yourself is better done sooner than later because once the manipulation continues for a long time, those manipulated begin to stop questioning and merely accept their new reality. They are the lemmings in this life, the zombies who walk about with feelings so buried they no longer have a sense of self. They are tossed about from one manipulator to another because they have changed their reality so many times they no longer have ownership in their lives.

In the following chapters, you will get insight into manipulation, mind control, and how to use NLP in a positive manner. So, here's to helping you

NEGOTIATION

change your perspective about manipulation and perhaps empower you to create a new reality of getting more of what you want and helping others to do the same.

CHAPTER 2

Step #1—Building Rapport vs. Fear

To practice positive manipulation, it's necessary to build rapport rather than strike fear in the minds of those you are manipulating. Not that fear won't do the job, but it's a harmful practice that will end up coming back to bite you in the behind. Contrary manipulators create fear in the minds of others, then play the hero, and immediately remove the fear with their manipulation. Fear is such a strong emotion that it quickly opens the doors of the mind for manipulation or mind control; however, the problem lies in the after effects. Fear doesn't necessarily allow you to change people's perspective and behavior; it is more of a short, immediate reaction that goes away once there's no longer any fear. Their reality hasn't changed. The old practices and behaviors are still lurking just below the surface—ready to resurface as soon as you alleviate the fear.

When you use fear to manipulate beliefs or behaviors, you don't create a long-lasting change in that person's reality. What you just might create is a long-term distrust. The people you are trying to manipulate will begin to associate you with their feelings of fear. Make no mistake, fear is one of the most powerful and efficient ways to manage people, and its results are immediate. The fortunate thing is that people who behave in a certain way out of fear, usually avoid the person and thereby the fear as well.

Results from Using the Fear Strategy to Manipulate

Since childhood, most of us have experienced fear manipulation. Our parents manipulated and controlled us by physical discipline or emotional blackmail, and our teachers managed us by threats and humiliation. Unfortunately, our perspectives and beliefs weren't changed at all, only our behaviors—and those changed only temporarily. What many learned by the time they were teenagers is that they didn't want to be around parents and teachers, and the friends or peers whose realities were similar became our closest network with the greatest amount of influence over them.

To illustrate this point, let's look at Raul. Raul entered the tenth-grade with a reputation for being a trouble-maker. He harassed all the girls in class, destroyed the classroom desks and books, and disrespected his teachers. When Raul tried his usual tactics with his English teacher, Miss Slater, she decided to call his father. Expecting that Raul's father would offer his support, she never dreamed he'd come down to the school and humiliate Raul in front of all his friends.

Unfortunately, Raul had to sit next to his father all day long as his father accompanied him to every class, pulling him by the ear from one room to another. Did it put the fear of God in him? I'm sure it did. Unfortunately, when the fear factor no longer held him hostage, Raul's behavior was even more disrespectful and threatening than before. He still harassed the girls in class, but now he warned

NEGOTIATION

them if they told he would meet them outside the classroom and make them sorry. What Raul's father had taught him was to manipulate through fear. Because Raul didn't experience positive manipulation, his reality was the same—act out and get all the attention you want. Since negative attention was all the attention Raul every experienced, he knew no better.

Not only did he continue to disrespect the girls in class, but he covertly sabotaged his teachers with practical jokes that were destructive and dangerous. He blew his nose and wiped the discharge between the pages of brand new textbooks. He keyed his teacher's car, and one day he sucked in the fumes from a butane lighter and blew them out as he lighted his breath. The fire was like a torch, catching the girl's hair on fire who sat in front of him. Instead of changing his behavior, practicing manipulation through fear hurt others and got him permanently expelled from school for the remainder of the year.

Comparing Fear Manipulation to Positive Rapport-Building Manipulative Attempts

The next year Raul returned, along with his reputation for being a rebellious bully. By now, his reality was "get them before they get me" school of thought. The fear manipulation hadn't achieved any beneficial changes in Raul's behaviors or perspective, except to reinforce the negative. What made matters worse is he was now a year behind his classmates and in danger of becoming another dropout statistic.

Fortunately for Raul, he got more than he bargained for in one of his new teachers, Mr. Thompson. Mr. Thompson was obviously a teacher who realized how to move and empower his students through positive manipulation; thereby, helping them to create a new reality for themselves. Raul came into the classroom with the same old mean-spirited, sour attitude, but instead of a write-up, after the reprimand, after another write-up, what Raul experienced was a teacher who believed in teaching through the continuous power of healthy relationships.

One day, both were in detention—Raul for disciplinary reasons from another hard-nosed

NEGOTIATION

teacher, and Mr. Thompson to act as supervisor for after-school detention. Mr. Thompson had a whole week of after-school detention time to build rapport with Raul. Mr. Thompson questioned Raul about his likes and dislikes, only to discover Raul's love for fast cars. Since Mr. Thompson's hobby was rebuilding an old muscle-car he had inherited from his great aunt, he decided to involve Raul in the process. He brought the car to school and stored it in the industrial arts building. Every day after school, Mr. Thompson and Raul would work on the car together.

Through his questions and rapport building, Mr. Thompson manipulated Raul to change his "get them before they get me" perspective on life. The improved behavior that began in Mr. Thompson's class soon spread to other aspects of Raul's life as well. As they finished the car, Mr. Thompson permitted Raul the privilege of taking dates out in his amazing muscle car. Girls had a new respect for Raul and his disrespectful attitude changed for them as well. Raul's mechanical talents surpassed that of Mr. Thompson, and he was often called to the house to assist him with needed repairs, strengthening their friendship and mutual respect.

Although it was a challenge to catch up, Raul passed that year with flying colors. As the years passed, he grew more confident and changed from rebellious to productive. His grades were good, and it was evident Raul had a real talent to repair anything mechanical. Toward the end of his senior year, Raul talked to Mr. Thompson about his inability to afford college and together they discussed other employment options. Graduation night, Raul had the biggest smile of any other student as he collected his diploma, knowing how hard he had worked and how many obstacles he had overcome with Mr. Thompson's help.

His mother and father had since divorced, and Raul's mom and younger brother were the only ones who cheered him on that evening. He searched the crowd for Mr. Thompson's familiar cheery face but was disappointed when he failed to see him in the line of teachers wishing their students good luck in their future endeavors. It was difficult for Raul to hid his disappointment as he

NEGOTIATION

slowly led his mother and brother down the front steps and out to the parking lot.

Raul felt so sorry for himself that he didn't see the bright red, 1965, convertible Mustang GTX at first until his mother touched his arm and spoke in a tearful voice. "Raul, I think Mr. Thompson has a surprise for you."

"I looked for him, but…"

"He's right there with your present."

There parked right in front of the steps was the car they had worked on for two years. It had a huge gold ribbon around it, with the words "Class of 1999" written on the window. Mr. Thompson was there to hand Raul the keys and wish him good luck in his future endeavors.

Today Raul owns a body shop, helps to support his mother and pays for his brother to attend the local junior college. That's the power of positive manipulation and Step #1 in our five steps.

Step #1—Building Rapport

It's a proven fact that people will do what you ask if you use fear or negative manipulation, but the real change happens when you build rapport and a positive relationship with them. That's what Mr. Thompson did with Raul. Let's look at how he manipulated Raul into changing his thinking, his perspective, his behaviors, and then helped him to create a new reality.

1. Discover Common Ground

    Mr. Thompson took the time to discover Raul's passion in life. What was it that got him excited? What would turn him on and plug him into life? At first, Raul spoke sarcastically about negative things, but he finally mentioned his love for fast cars. Here was something that Raul and Mr. Thompson had in common. Easy conversation not Raul's first response to Mr. Thompson's questions; it took some digging to find some common ground in which Mr. Thompson could begin to manipulate Raul to move in another direction positively.

    So, asking questions is necessary to find the first building-block of rapport, and it takes rapport to establish substantial grounds for manipulation.

2. Change the Focus

Instead of harping on Raul about his bad behavior or poor grades, Mr. Thompson began to talk about cars with Raul. Soon, Raul turned his focus from belligerently spouting off about things he hated to calming discussing things he felt passionate about with Mr. Thompson. Bottom line, Mr. Thompson manipulated Raul to change his emotional state from negative to positive, and in doing so, he got Raul to begin thinking about positive outcomes resulting from his changed behaviors. If Raul worked hard and got the car running—if he performed well in school—if he were more respectful to girls, then he would get to drive the car he helped to rebuild. Instead of focusing on what he couldn't do, Raul began to measure his new reality by what he could do.

3. Approval and Acceptance

Whenever Mr. Thompson showed approval and acceptance of Raul's behavior, it strengthened the young man's resolve to continue along that same path. Raul began to enjoy the positive attention, praise, and encouragement. Not only did he meet Mr. Thompson's expectations, but Raul exceeded them. His previous reality of "get them before they get me," was now changing to "do more for them than they do for me."

4. Reinforce the New Behavior

Mr. Thompson then continued the positive manipulation by reinforcing Raul's budding new reality. They made an agreement; if Raul continued to do well in school and be respectful, he could take his dates out in the Mustang. What a thrill it was for Raul. For the first time, Raul got more attention from being respectful than he did from being physically and emotionally abusive. The better he behaved, the more positive reinforcement he received.

5. Reward the Change

NEGOTIATION

Most of us think of Raul's big prize as the Mustang, but that was not the final win. What changed Raul's reality for life was all the positive he brought to others from his changed perspective and behavior. Appreciation and thanks from his brother and mother were Raul's continued rewards. The business Raul built as a result of all his hard work was a reward. Mr. Thompson's positive manipulation that created an entirely new reality and offered him a future he could never have imagined possible was Raul's final prize.

These are the five components of Step #1 — Building Rapport vs. fear. Fear manipulation changed nothing for Raul, but positive manipulation through building rapport changed his life. Not only was Raul rewarded, but Mr. Thompson's life was changed for the better as well. He and Raul remained good friends, and he learned the difference a teacher could make in the life of a young person. He learned exceptional manipulation skills that he still practices today to move his students to peak performance in the classroom and life.

CHAPTER 3

Step #2—Defining Desired Outcomes

I'm sure you've heard that the best negotiations are a win/win for everyone, right? Well, the same holds true for manipulation. The more valid form of manipulations is in which everybody wins. It's like a good relationship; if one person does all the taking and another all the giving, the relationship isn't going to last. When practicing the most efficient and effective forms of manipulation, if both parties don't feel as though they benefited, the desired outcome will not be achieved. To know what it will take to make you and the other person feel like winners, you need to know what you want and what they want.

NEGOTIATION

What Do You Want for Your Desired Outcome?

If you don't define your desired outcomes, how will you know when you have achieved your goals and helped them to accomplish theirs as well? As important as it was to ask your subject questions to build rapport, it's just as important to ask yourself questions to determine what you want. The following are some suggested questions that will help you identify your desired outcome. If you think you know what your desired outcome is, question further to determine if this is your passionate desire.

For illustration purposes, let's imagine that your desired outcome was to lead the top-performing team in your workplace. However, to achieve this desired result, you need buy-in from the other team members. First, test your stated desired outcome to make sure it is your passion. If you are not passionate about your desired outcome, you cannot manipulate others to your way of thinking and behaving. Your team may do well, but your reality of leading the top performing team at work will probably not happen. The following questions will enable you to test your level of passion.

1. How will leading the top performing team in my workplace change my reality?

2. What will I experience in this changed reality that I cannot experience now?

3. What will I need to do to make my desired outcome a reality?

4. Am I willing to do what was listed in #3 to attain my desired result?

5. How will the rest of my team benefit when I manipulate them to my way of thinking?

Once you have successfully examined the answers to these questions, and everything still points to a win/win for everyone involved, you're ready to begin your manipulations to move the other team members to greater production and performance.

What Desired Outcomes Do You Want for Those You are Manipulating?

There's only one thing you want for them, and that is for them to benefit from doing what you want them to do. You already know what you need the

NEGOTIATION

subject of your manipulations to do, how to think and behave, and now what you want for them is to jump on board. The problem is, they're less likely to be manipulated to your way of thinking if it doesn't turn them on, if they cannot relate to your desired outcome, or if they are not passionate about what you want for them.

Let's face it, you know they would be better off if their work performance was top-notch. You know all team players would feel better about themselves and be more likely to be promoted or receive bonuses if they were members of the top performing team, right? And, that is your desired outcome for you and them. Now, what you must do is determine what gives each one an immediate payoff to persuade them to seek that position as top performing team. It's the instant gratification that will get the team's attention and manipulate them to participate in your desired outcome.

That's where the rapport building skills come in handy. You need to build rapport with every member of your team and discover what each person's payoff will be before they are "all in" to move toward your desired outcome. Don't think it's always going to be money, either. Here are some primary motivators that manipulators use to move people to their desired outcome.

- Friendship
- Recognition
- Power
- Wealth
- Position
- Praise
- Belonging
- Material Possessions
- Fame
- Prestige
- Envy of Others
- Help Family

- For the Fun

- Challenge

- Emotional and Physical Well-Being

Making Your Manipulation All About Others

Manipulation is entirely different from convincing people on your ideas. People don't want you to "sell" them on your desired outcome; they want to attain their desired outcome through their individual ideas and efforts. What needs to happen for long-term manipulation to occur is that others have total buy-in to your desired outcome. In fact, before completing your manipulations, your desired outcome and theirs should be the same. That's a real reality change that will last the test of time.

Think of the wants and needs of those whom you are manipulating as your hook to get their attention and real them in to come to your desired outcome. It is still done in a positive manner—not by fear, intimidation, or humiliation. Using the same example of the team of co-workers, let's examine the five things you can do to get them to help you achieve your desired outcome and still reward them for their efforts.

1. Instead of focusing on what they are doing wrong, focus on what you are doing right. Talk about how rewarding it has been to be privileged enough to lead the group and how you plan to make the team the top-performers in the company. State your desired outcome as a team effort. Include them in your plans for the entire team to be successful. Praise them, perhaps telling them that you are happy you are a part of their team. They are hand-chosen for success. Of course, this is also true for other situations of manipulations. Always involve the ones you are manipulating with your plans of success.

2. Model the behavior and beliefs you wish them to have to achieve your desired outcome. It does little good to expect others to participate in your desired outcome if you don't give it your all as well. Those you want to manipulate will want to please you, so make sure you are modeling the behavior and perceptions you want from

NEGOTIATION

them. If you expect them to give it 150 percent, then you do the same. If you expect your team members to work until the project gets done, then you be there right along with them.

If this is not a work project, but someone with whom you are in a relationship with that you wish to manipulate, then you must model your expectations. If you want them to listen to you, then you must be willing to hear them as well. If you want them to be more responsive to your needs, then you need to be more sensitive to their needs. That's the way everybody wins — everybody benefits from your desired outcome.

3. Assume all members are already on board with your ideas. Assumptions are an essential element to manipulating others. Don't ask for their opinions or ideas, believe theirs is the same as yours. If someone expresses an opposing view, let them know you value their input, and their concerns are quite insightful. Then, explain how those very concerns are addressed with your plan. Gain acceptance and approval by encouraging them to state how they have

already benefited from the changes that have taken place. If you become a dictator and tell someone what to think, they can always deny or doubt the validity of what you say. However, if you manipulate the situation in a way that convinces them to state their agreement, then those you are manipulating are not going to doubt their stated beliefs.

4. Talk and act as if you are already the top performing team in the company. The more you do, the more your team members will adopt this attitude as well. If you want to manipulate someone into being more responsible, give them more trust and let them prove their responsibility. If people want to have more privileges, then they should demonstrate responsibility first. What about you? Do you believe this statement? In truth, the reverse is true. If you want people to be more accountable, give them more privileges and let them demonstrate their responsibility.

Do you hear how the two views are slightly different? I'm sure you've heard parents say to

NEGOTIATION

their children "You disobeyed me; there will be no more privileges until you can earn back my trust." Really? How can that happen when the child has little opportunity to do so? In our reality, things happen just the other way around. Okay, we're going to give you this privilege, and "assume" you will be trustworthy.

5. When you have observed a team-member going above and beyond the others, give plenty of public recognition and praise. Soon, others on the team will want the same for themselves. Everybody likes to be valued and appreciated.

There was a young mother who always complained that her son wouldn't do his chores, and when he did decide to do some work around the house it was never right, and he still wanted to get paid his allowance. Until she learned how to manipulate his behavior and perceptions, her son continued to display a rather lazy attitude with the unreasonable expectations of being paid for nothing.

So, how did she manipulate her son into defining a new reality? First, she asked and expected nothing of him. His younger brother continued to do his chores, was given praise and recognition, and paid his usual allowance in front of his older brother at the end of the week. The mother showed affection to her older son as well, but he was not praised or recognized for chores that he had not done. She would mention her younger son's achievements to the father as he came home from work, and the father would also acknowledge the younger brother's good behavior in the presence of his older son. Nothing negative was said or done to punish the older child, but there was no display of pleasure for work he did not do.

In just over a week, the older son wanted in on the positive rewards, as well as the allowance. He eagerly completed his daily chores and did a good job. The mother's desired outcome for her son was for him to do his chores without complaining, and do them to her standards. She also made an agreement with her oldest son that she would not nag him to do his chores; it was his choice. If he wanted his allowance, then the assigned tasks would need to be done.

The surprise in her manipulation was when she had forgotten to give her son his allowance, and he had forgotten to ask for it. His beliefs, behaviors, and perspective had changed so drastically that his motivation was no longer the money, but the reward was the recognition and praise. The beauty of positive manipulation is that everybody wins.

Manipulation Takes Consistency, Control, and Focus

The more challenging the desired outcome for you and others, the more consistency, control and focus it requires from the manipulator. Remember, you need to model the behavior. Passion and patience are necessary to achieve your goal and help others change their reality to align with your desires. Modeling your outcome needs to be an exaggeration of what you want others to do. For example, let's say your desired outcome is for there to be no swearing or yelling in your home. You don't' want your husband or children to swear—

not one word. You don't even want your company and friends to curse when they are visiting.

The obvious first step is to let everybody know that you would like your home to be a swear-free zone. Next, you are the first one to clean up your language. That means no swearing by you in the presence of your husband or children, or even when you think they can't hear you. No swearing. Next, you let them know how much calmer you feel when you're not resorting to swearing. Assume you hear no swearing, and comment on how good it feels not to let frustration get the best of you.

Every time you want to swear but resist the temptation, give a little giggle and say how you're not going to swear. Cheerfully comment on how good it is not to let your immature emotions get the best of you. When you notice less swearing in the house, you praise your family on controlling their language. To continue the manipulation, mention how much happier everybody is with less swearing and verbal frustration in the house. When someone uses a substitute word where they would have previously sworn, make a joke of it and let them

NEGOTIATION

know how clever they are to have thought of using that word.

Point out the peacefulness and calm you feel, and how grown up it is to see your children control their frustration and emotions. Don't be surprised if your children's friends swear in the house and you don't have to correct them. You've done such a good job manipulating your kids that they'll admonish their friends for the swearing and let them know your home is now a swear-free zone.

All this fuss over swearing might seem silly to many of you, but it's a way to practice your manipulation methods. Try manipulation on smaller things first, and then move on to bigger issues when you have honed your skills. Be sure that you are just as passionate about the desired outcomes on the smaller things, or you won't be successful. Your passion for changing other's reality is what drives you to achieve the desired results.

CHAPTER 4

Step #3—Considering the Consequences

Every action has a consequence, whether you choose to accept it or not. We are all so connected, that what you do directly affects the behaviors and actions of others. There is no better reason to act and behave responsibly regarding manipulation. If you do believe that we are connected, then should you choose to manipulate another in a negative way, you are bringing all the negative consequences right back on yourself. For this reason, you must consider the consequences of your behaviors and decisions when you are manipulating others. Step #3 is one of the most important ones to reaching your desired outcome.

NEGOTIATION

If you have done your homework before manipulating others, you are acutely aware of the first consequence of your actions. Most of you have researched and weighed what you want that desired outcome to be, and you prepare yourself for the consequences of your actions. However, what surprises you is that most manipulative activities have secondary effects that may not evolve until much later. The secondary effects seem to happen so randomly that you fail to connect these new behaviors or beliefs with your original action.

The United States unemployment benefits is an excellent example of delayed consequences that nobody considered would be the direct result of manipulation. Originally designed to help people who had lost their jobs or were out of work for a short period, unemployment, the government intervened and offered compensation until people could re-train themselves and get back on their feet. While this worked in the beginning, the result we see in our current society is not quite so positive. Many of today's workers have learned how to manipulate the system, creating a reality that is not quite what the government had counted on happening. Instead of unemployment compensation helping people who are out of work, it has held them back from returning to the workforce and becoming productive citizens.

Instead of collecting unemployment for a short period while they are actively seeking a job, many people discover how long they can receive the benefits to which they feel entitled. Instead of trying to find a job immediately, they live off unemployment pay until it is down to zero. However, the secondary consequences continue even further. With these unemployed workers' prolonged absences from the workplace, different skills, and systems progress. Now they are no longer qualified or knowledgeable enough to compete with their peers. The money has run out, so they can no longer collect unemployment benefits at a time when they need the financial help.

What happens now is an endless cycle of governmental handouts, which was not a part of the government's desired outcomes? The unemployed soon move from unemployment benefits to Welfare, which was also only designed to help in a temporary capacity. The unintended consequences of these programs are that we now have generations of family members whose new reality is one where they were born and had lived most of their lives surviving the only way they know how—on Welfare. Although it was not the intent of the program, life-long Welfare recipients are cheated out of significant accomplishments because they grew up in a broken system as a result of unintentional consequences.

Nothing Comes without a Cost

When you decide to manipulate others, you must take responsibility for the new reality you help to create. If that reality wasn't quite what you bargained for, then the problem might have been that you didn't carefully consider the consequences of your actions. Here are some questions to ask yourself when thinking through the consequences that could occur because of your manipulations.

1. What will happen to myself and others if I manipulate this person?

2. What will happen to myself and others if I choose not to manipulate this person?

3. If I do nothing to manipulate the desired outcome, what happens?

4. If I do nothing to manipulate the outcome you want, what will not occur?

5. Will I and others be harmed if I do not manipulate the desired outcome?

6. Will I and others benefit from my manipulations?

7. Knowing there will be a cost, am I willing to take full responsibility for my manipulations?

8. Knowing that I could have positively affected the desired outcome, am I willing to take full liability for choosing not to manipulate the situation?

If everything comes with a cost, that means doing nothing also has its consequences. If you decide not to manipulate others, it might mean that you will not achieve your desired outcomes and nor will they. Are you willing to accept the consequences if you say no to the benefits that could happen if you were ready to follow the steps in this book and positively manipulate the other person? If you are still stuck on the belief that manipulating others is wrong, then you need to change your perception which will result in a new reality. Once you learn that manipulation can be rewarding, you'll wonder why you ever thought differently.

Accepting the Consequences is Empowering

Knowing that your actions and decisions have a profound effect on yourself and others is quite empowering. When you accept this reality, you are aware that you are in control of your destiny. If you want to manipulate your reality, then act and make that change happen. If you want to help others create a new reality, then you have the power to manipulate that situation to bring about for them a more positive desired outcome and a new reality that leads them to a better life. Knowing these truths about manipulation encourages you never to use manipulation to harm others because you would ultimately be doing harm to yourself and negatively change your reality as well.

Realizing the difference one person can make in the lives of many is a daunting consideration. Along with that come the "what if" concerns, such as "What if I make a mistake in my decision to manipulate?" Or, "What if the desired outcome is far from what I counted on and it hurts others?" These are real concerns, and you're right to play the "what if" game. If you learn to manipulate others, you are going to experience the consequences of bad decisions or poorly planned manipulation. There will be a time when someone gets hurt by your manipulations or a time when you don't achieve your desired outcome.

Nothing ventured—nothing gained is a rule that many manipulators adopt to be in charge of their future. If they decide never to manipulate others, then they will not experience all the benefits manipulation offers. What's worse, those who could have benefited will also lose the opportunity for a better life. All because you let fear stop you.

NEGOTIATION

There's something about the fear you should know! You fear what you don't understand—what you don't know. It's natural to fear manipulation. First, you already have some preconceived ideas that perhaps aren't so positive about manipulation, so you've built the wall that you'll now have to scale. If you are empowered enough to create a whole new reality for yourself, you can also create enough fear to block success. It sounds perverse, but your fear of manipulation is manipulating you.

Fear is a self-imposed false belief, so your fearful reality is based on false facts. Decisions based on a false premise are not sound. That's why Step #1 in this book was about getting rid of the fear. You can't expect others to follow you if you fear the outcome. Chances are, the consequences you might experience from a poor decision are much lighter than the results you live now because you're bowing down to fear. It's not that you will never be fearful to move forward, but being an outstanding manipulator means you confidently pursue your desired result no matter what. If you begin manipulations with a wishy-washy belief, and your behaviors are On-again/off-again, your manipulations will fail. You'll disappoint those you want to help. Instead of letting the fear paralyze you, learn to push past it and scale that wall to a favorable desired result.

When Your Manipulations Aren't Working

Don't wait until the cows come home to change things up a little bit. When your efforts are coming to a stalemate, make some minor adjustments to your plan of action. The fact is when you begin manipulating others it doesn't seem like a very positive experience. The more others have been programmed to believe and behave in a particular way, the more resistant they are and the less ground you can cover. For a while, you might try making a few little changes. Nothing major, just some small adjustments to your behaviors. If several minor changes in your plan don't create marked progress in your manipulation, it's time to shake things up with a radical change.

Making a radical change to force another's hand will usually accomplish one of two outcomes. Either you lose the opportunity to manipulate the other person, which you probably would have done anyway without a radical change; or, you will shake them out of their rut, and they'll begin moving forward to your desired outcome. Making a radical change acts as a wake-up call to those you are manipulating. It's like dumping ice water on the face of a sleeping person. You're going to wake them up for sure, and then they have a decision to make. Do they go for you, or do they laugh it off and start their day? At this point, it can go either way. What won't happen is another unproductive day where your manipulation goes nowhere, and your desired outcome gets further away until it seems to be out of reach.

Learning to Manipulate Is Not for the Faint of Heart

It takes courage to manage others. After all, you're the one taking risks, putting your reputation on the line, and leading another person or group to a better life. It's a battle of wills, and leaders in combat are the first to be injured if their plan of attack is flawed. On the other hand, leaders also reap the highest rewards. There's nothing like manipulating a situation where you get what you want, others get what they want, and you were directly responsible for the accomplishment. It's even better when others recognize you as the one who made it all happen, so don't be shy about tooting your own horn. It's a great way to set yourself up for the next time you need to manipulate the situation. Everybody likes to follow a proven winner.

If you're feeling fearful, don't give up because you think you don't have the courage to continue. Brave manipulators feel fear, they feel defeated, and they feel like giving up, but the difference is they don't give into their fears. They continue to do what they know will bring them greater opportunities for success. They continue to move people to do the same with their lives, even when the odds are against them.

CHAPTER 5

STEP #4—BE THE SOLUTION TO THEIR PROBLEM

It's difficult to manipulate people when they don't feel there is a need for change. Creating that need is paramount in your ability to control and manage the situation and get what you want. The people you want to manipulate always have needs and wants, so it's up to you to discover their needs and then prove to them you are the answer. Instead of thinking of what they want as a need, consider that need to be a problem. It's either a problem they have or a problem caused by what they don't have.

I can hear the wheels turning in your head about right now. You're probably saying to yourself, but what if their need isn't a real problem? Don't go there; think of it as a problem, and it will make your manipulation easier to set up, even if the problem is a good one to have.

To demonstrate this method, let's create a scenario where you are a real estate agent, and you want to manipulate your prospects into purchasing a home. The prospects visit your community, and the exchange goes something like this.

Step #1—Building Rapport

Remember, you cannot manipulate until you have built rapport, so here are some of the things you'll want to do to build rapport.

- Smile and get up out of your chair to greet them.

  There's nothing worse when you're visiting a new home community to have someone sitting in their office who's too lazy to greet you and thank you for coming in to see them. Waving them through to the models is more likely to build an enemy than a friend.

- Next, you'll introduce yourself and get their name.

NEGOTIATION

It might sound something like this as you offer your hand. "Hi, my name is Linda—and you are…?" Most people will tell you their names. If they don't tell you their names then you can always say: "I'm so bad with names. What did you say your first name was?" Do this after you've made some small talk and gained their trust.

Continue to make casual conversation until the prospects relax. If you can get them to laugh, you're well on your way. Once you have learned their names, use them. Everybody likes to hear their name. Not too much or it will sound manipulative, just pepper the conversation here and there with their names.

Step #2—Defining Desired Outcomes

During Step #2, you'll be asking lots of questions to discover what they want. Of course, when you ask them what they are looking for in a new home, the standard answer will be "Well, we need a three bedroom, two-bath home." Since that's not very enticing, and you know that's the standard answer, you might come back with a laugh and say, "Okay, soooo—let me get this straight. If I have a three bedroom, two-bath home to sell you today, you'll be ready to buy, right?"

Of course, they are going to laugh at you, and then you begin to dig a little more. To discover the reason the prospects are out looking for a new home, you continue to ask more questions that make them think a little. It might sound like this: "So, Joan, when you and Ken were sitting over dinner talking about the new home you would love to own, how did that home look? If this were your perfect dream home, what would it look like?" Now you've got them thinking; they're more engaged in the conversation.

Step #3—Considering the Consequences

On this next step in your attempts to manipulate the prospects, you engage their imagination and help them to see the consequences of their decision. What would their life be like if they moved, or what would their life be like if they decided not to move? When you engage a person's imagination, don't be afraid to ask them to play along. It might sound like this. "Joan and Ken, I'm going to ask you to pretend with me for a moment. If you decided not to purchase a home and instead stay in the home you are currently living in, what would your life be like—let's say, for the next year?"

You always want to put a timeframe on that question to keep them focused on the immediacy or urgency of their decision. Now is when you're going to get to the "problem." Let's say your prospects said something like this. "Well, it would be difficult for us to stay in our current home because we just found out Joan is pregnant and we're going to need more space. Okay, that's a problem, but it's still going to take some more questions to determine whether this is the most pressing issue, or if there is another underlying issue.

For example, the prospects might need more space as well, but the real problem might be that they don't want to raise their child in that neighborhood, or in that school district. Whatever the issue may be, it might take some more flushing out with continued questioning. It's common that people don't disclose their problem early on in a relationship. They need time to develop trust.

Okay, let's say the real problem was that they need more space for their growing family. What you need to do in your manipulations now, is to expand the problem. Blow it way out of proportion, as if you were blowing up a balloon. Your next questions might be as follows:

- "Do you have enough property to add another bedroom onto your current home?"

   (Let's say they cannot add another bedroom.)

- "So, if you were to stay in your current home for the next year, what would your life be like?"

   (The prospects begin to tell you how difficult it would be to grow their family and stay in this tiny home.)

- Now, comes more manipulation. Remember when we discussed that you cannot dictate or tell a person what they need because they will doubt it when YOU say it? It's critical at this point to get the prospects to say they need to

NEGOTIATION

purchase a home, and that's so much easier than what you could imagine. All you need to do is ask this one little question and frame it this way.

"So, if you have no space to add a bedroom, and you are going to need the extra room, or it's going to be difficult to get around in your tiny house, what is it that you need to do?" After you ask this question, you stop talking. The next thing that happens is the prospects give you the answer you want to hear. They say, "Well, I guess we'll need to make a move."

Once you've manipulated the conversation and got the prospects to see their need or "problem," all you must to do is be the solution to their problem. The manipulation was getting the people to say what you wanted to hear. As in every plan, you know what success will look and sound like, so you need to move the person into ownership of their problem. They must voice what you want as if it were their idea.

Step #4 — Be the Solution to their Problem

The reason I went through the first three steps before discussing Step #4 is so that you could see the manipulation sequence. It is easier to follow when you see the progression of your manipulation. When you are manipulating the person to see you as the solution to their problem, you must show them how you and your ideas or plan or perceptions are superior to anyone else's. What makes you stand out from the crowd? To give yourself that notable difference and your manipulation a winning boost, you need to listen to what they say they want and observe their responses to your probing questions. When they look excited about something you've said, file that in your memory. If they seem agitated when you are probing for more information, keep in mind what you were discussing when they showed their discomfort.

Being smart about how you set yourself apart will help you manipulate the people or situation and get what you want while helping them also achieve their goal. If what you are proposing doesn't help them solve their problem, then you haven't succeeded. You haven't reached your desired outcome. Instead of being the solution to their problem, you may have created a whole other issue. Even if you are the solution to their problem, but you haven't made yourself indispensable, then they won't recognize you as having the solution.

There could be many ways to solve their problem, but your manipulations should convince them that your way is the best way. You don't have to prove that you have the solution, all you need to do is manipulate their perception. The idea that you are the solution to their problem is merely a mindset. People believe what they want to believe, so your job is to make them want to believe in you. If you've had success with the other three steps, then coming to an agreement that you have the solution is just the natural culmination of your manipulation.

Empathetic Manipulation

Empathetic manipulation is a gray area because it is so easy to play upon one's emotions, which can move you into selfish and negative manipulation that is designed to benefit nobody but yourself. Remember what we said about this type of manipulation? In the end, everybody loses, including you. If you use empathetic manipulation to the detriment of others, you will eventually lose their trust and friendship. Having said this, if you decide to be empathetic when you are manipulating others, do so with caution. A little goes a long way.

In the case of the new homes salesperson, he or she could safely let the prospects know their problem was common and he would help them find a solution, but to display false emotions or deep caring that isn't real is taking unfair advantage. If you pretend to be the solution to their problem when, in fact, you know you are not, your manipulation will fail or be only a brief blip on the screen of their reality. Not only that, but this kind of pretense is often transparent, even to the most naïve.

Knowing that people make decisions emotionally and justify them logically, it's important that you identify and understand the emotions they feel. However, it is harmful manipulation when you prey upon their emotions to get them to follow you like little zombies. If you have real empathy for

NEGOTIATION

them, your manipulations will be fair and just. You can show your compassion by being understanding and then continue to manipulate them if you know it will be to their benefit. Unfortunately, if during the time of managing them you discover something that you know will hurt them if you continue, it's time to stop. Manipulations over!

CHAPTER 6

STEP #5—ASSUMING SUCCESS

You may think your focus is on success, but it could be of worry and anxiety about not getting what you want. Studies have shown that people who focus on what they want are more likely to achieve their goals. However, the focus must be on what you want, not what you don't want. Although that sounds easy enough, let's illustrate the difference. Pretend your significant other has a cold, and you don't want to catch it. You believe in the power of positive thought and affirmations, so your plan is to focus on not getting a cold. Several times a day you say to yourself "I will not catch this cold. I will not catch this cold."

Here's the problem. This mindset or perspective is just the opposite of where you should focus.

Instead of focusing on good health, you're focused on the cold. If you want to practice positive affirmations, what you should be saying to yourself is "I am healthy and vigorous. I am healthy, active, and full of energy." See the difference? One statement keeps your mind centered on the cold, while the other keeps you focused on good health and an active body. The reason positive affirmations don't work for a lot of people is that the affirmations aren't so positive.

The Strongest Voice in your Life is Your Own

The best way to analyze if you are assuming success and focusing on the positive is to analyze your self-talk. What does that little voice in your head say to you all the time? Have you been positively focused on achieving your desired outcome, or does your self-talk sound something like this: "I don't want my son to take drugs anymore." Or, "I want to stop smoking and have the rest of my family quit as well." What is your mind focused on right now? Smoking, right?

How can you manipulate your thoughts to change your focus and achieve your desired outcome? The quickest way is to change your self-talk to this. "I eat healthily, drink plenty of water, watch what I put in my mouth, and have clear lungs." Instead of smoking, your focus is on being healthy.

Translating this to assuming success, you need to examine your self-talk during the times you are moving forward to achieve your desired outcome. Let's pretend you want your husband to stop using the credit card so much and get it paid down to zero. You've given it lots of thought, and you focus on being out of debt. You have talked to your husband about your desires and asked him not to use the credit card. You've even tried to manipulate the situation through praise and reward for not using the card. You've heard about the power of visualization, so you've visualized the amount on your credit card getting lower and lower each day. Okay, now here's my question. How would you feel if that's what happened—if you paid the credit card in full? Would you be pleasantly surprised?

I hope you got the issues with this way of thinking. Let's look at your focus.

NEGOTIATION

1. You imagined your husband not using the credit card instead of imagining a wallet full of cash to pay for your wanted items. Even though you stated you wanted your husband to stop using the credit card, your focus was still on the card.

2. You next said that your focus would be to get out of debt. Still, instead of an emphasis on a positive cash flow and all the money you have in the bank, your focus is on your debt. You have assumed debt to be in your future.

3. You then pass on your negative focus on not using the credit card to your husband, and his thoughts fuel the fire. Why? Because now you have two minds concentrated on the credit card. Praise and reward were even given to strengthen your thinking about the credit card.

4. Now you visualize the amount on the credit card getting lower, instead of your cash flow getting stronger.

5. When asked how you would feel if that happened, did you catch the most important word in the sentence? It was the elephant in the room—the "IF." If you were assuming success that word would have been "WHEN" not "IF."

6. Lastly, when asked if you were pleasantly surprised--if you always assume success there should never be a surprise when getting what you want. Your success was no accident—it was the achievement of a chosen desired outcome.

There has been much discussion on manipulating others to change their perspective, but before you can do that, you might need to change your thinking as well. Always assume success. Every thought you have should lead you to your desired outcome. Every word spoken should focus your mind on what you want. Every action should move you closer to your goal. Instead of hoping you will achieve your goal—expect success.

NEGOTIATION

Manipulating Your Thoughts to Focus on Success

There are three easy things you can do to control your thoughts and direct them on a path to success.

1. Focus on what you want, not on what you'll need to stop doing or start doing to get what you want. If you want to lose weight, visualize yourself as thin and beautiful. If you want to purchase a new car, don't focus on saving the money. Keep your eyes on the prize and envision yourself driving that new car.

2. Get out the doubt. Think "WHEN" not "IF." Assume success by acting as if you already have what you want.

3. Lead without looking back. Expect others to follow your lead, because they will. When you lead with confidence and conviction, they will follow. When you lead with weakness and doubt, they will follow that as well.

The Driving Force for Success

The driving force for success is passion. If you are not passionate about your purpose, then how will you successfully manipulate others to assist in achieving your desired outcome? The thing about a great mindset is that it's highly contagious. Those who you are manipulating will mimic your mood and feelings, so make sure they are confident and powerful. Having a passion for your desired outcome is this.

P = Practicing positive self-talk

A = Assuming success

S = Set your expectations

S = Search every alternative

I = Identify your desired outcome

O = Offer the best solution to others

N = Nothing can stop you from getting what you want!

NEGOTIATION

When you are passionate about what you want, you naturally talk excitedly about it, and your enthusiasm attracts others to your cause. Those you can most easily manipulate may not be the first to join in; past people who practiced harmful manipulation on them made them wary of your intentions. You might have to reach out to them a little more. However, once your passion has spread, they'll be your most loyal champions. They continue to spread the word, like little ambassadors of your ideas. The nurturing and reassuring may take more energy, but it will be well worth it.

Without even realizing it, you'll soon be practicing NLP. Your thoughts and focus will change, your language will change, and you'll be able to use past programming to mold your future and that of those you are manipulating. Sound manipulation is when everybody wins!

CONCLUSION

Thank you for purchasing *Manipulation: The Complete Step-by-Step Guide on Manipulation, Mind Control, and NLP.*

I hope this book will help you to get what you want by applying our step-by-step strategies on achieving your desired outcome through positive manipulation. Success isn't always immediate, but as you learn the art of positive focus and develop single-minded determination to get what you want, others will be attracted to your success. Using the five steps presenting in this book will help you manipulate the beliefs and behaviors of others, and change their reality right along with yours.

The next step is to practice our step-by-step guide to successful manipulations. When you master these steps, you can achieve success in your personal relationships, career goals, and attain those material things you've always dreamed of owning. To manipulate successfully, you need to focus and be passionate about your goals. People will follow your lead, whether you are confident and excited or weak and doubtful. How you manipulate is as important as who you manipulate.

Finally, if you enjoyed this book, you'll want to read some of my other works, such as *Manipulation: The Definitive Guide to Understanding Manipulation, Mind Control, and NLP,* and *Manipulation Mastery: How to Master Manipulation, Mind Control, and NLP.* You'll gain even more insight into the wonders of manipulating others to get them to help you achieve success. Making sure everybody wins is paramount to sustained success in your manipulations.

I'd like to ask you one last favor; if you enjoyed reading the book, please take time to share your views with us by posting a review. It'd be highly appreciated! Having a positive review from you will help this book reach many more people, so that they can benefit from the information shared within this book as well.

Thank you and good luck on all your future manipulations!

www.ingramcontent.com/pod-product-compliance
Lightning Source LLC
Chambersburg PA
CBHW052057110526
44591CB00013B/2255